Original title:
The Vulture's View

Copyright © 2024 Swan Charm
All rights reserved.

Editor: Jessica Elisabeth Luik
Author: Eliora Lumiste
ISBN HARDBACK: 978-9916-86-505-7
ISBN PAPERBACK: 978-9916-86-506-4

Bygone Baleful

In the whispers of forgotten years,
Shadows dance in moonlit veils.
Echoes of unfinished tears,
In hollow halls where silence prevails.

Ancient sorrow brews unseen,
Whispered secrets, lies untold.
Memory's grip like evergreen,
Their tendrils clutch the young and old.

Ghostly threads of time's descent,
Weave through hearts with ageless pain.
Chasing down the dreams we've spent,
In a life's ephemeral chain.

From the ashes of despair,
Rise the flames of yesterday.
Lingering in twilight's glare,
They guide the frail and lead astray.

Yet in the dawn where light emerges,
Hope's frail whisper begs to call.
Beyond the night's most somber dirges,
Awaits a promise to enthrall.

Ambassador of Ash

Carrying the weight of shattered dreams,
Through the realms of fire and frost.
In his gaze, a thousand themes,
Chronicled by what was lost.

Walking paths where shadows hum,
With each step, a tale is spun.
Silent is the ash-bound drum,
Beating for the lost and won.

Guardian of forgotten flames,
Burnished wings of soot and grief.
Bearing names, unspoken claims,
His silence speaks in stark relief.

Beneath the sky of endless night,
Eyes reflect the ember's gleam.
Guiding souls by candlelight,
Through the tendrils of a dream.

Where the sun no longer shines,
And past and future intertwine.
Ashen words in tangled lines,
Reveal the legacy of time.

Hunter's Paragon

In shadows deep, where twilight fades,
The hunter stalks in silent glades.
With keenest eye and steady hand,
He masters night by his command.

Tracks and whispers, silent screams,
Guide his steps through moonlit dreams.
Beast and prey, a deadly dance,
In forest's heart, he takes his chance.

Nature's balance, life's cruel jest,
The hunter proves his mettle best.
In every breath, a fleeting song,
Where he belongs, the wild, lifelong.

Twilight Spectator

In the hush of evening's grace,
A spectator finds their place.
Where shadows weave with fading light,
They watch the world embrace the night.

Stars awaken, whispers bloom,
Painting skies in soft perfume.
A cosmic dance above the earth,
The twilight sings of day's rebirth.

Each moment passing, transient glow,
Leaves a mark on hearts below.
In stillness, they see past the veil,
Where dreams and silent specters sail.

Purveyor of Ruin

Amid the echoes of lost abound,
The purveyor of ruin makes his round.
With every step, terrain decays,
Turning vibrant life to ashen grays.

His touch is death, his breath despair,
No thriving leaf, no verdant fair.
Structures crumble, hopes dissolve,
Beneath his gaze, all woes revolve.

Yet from the ashes, whispers rise,
Of new beginnings, whispered ties.
Through ruin, cycles still persist,
With every end, a chance exists.

Ghostly Wingspan

Beneath the moon's pale, eerie gleam,
A ghostly creature takes its theme.
With wings like mist and silent flight,
It haunts the edges of the night.

Its presence felt, a chilling breeze,
Whispers through the ancient trees.
In shadows cast, it finds its way,
Through realms where light begins to sway.

Eternal wanderer, spirit guide,
Across the astral planes it glides.
In spectral silence, stories weave,
Of times that mortal minds conceive.

Celestial Scavenger

In the expanse of night, it glides,
A shadow against the moonlit tides.
Stars whisper secrets as it seeks,
Ancient echoes the silence speaks.

Wings of dark velvet spread so wide,
Across galaxy's reach, it will bide.
Collecting shards of cosmic tales,
On a journey where no light fails.

Planets like jewels in its gaze,
Myth and mystery it appraises.
Constellations mark its keen quest,
Among the heavens, it finds its nest.

Death's Emissary

Silent harbinger cloaked in gray,
Herald of the end, come what may.
A whisper in the wind's soft sigh,
Guiding souls when it's time to fly.

Eyes cold as a winter's stare,
Yet a heart that shows tender care.
Through shadowed paths it strides alone,
Leading spirits to the unknown.

No terror in the steps it takes,
Only peace in the form it makes.
A comfort in the closing door,
As life fades, it brings evermore.

Vigil in the Heights

On mountain peaks where eagles soar,
A lonely watcher, evermore.
Scanning horizons far and wide,
Guarding secrets the winds confide.

Silent sentinel of the night,
In twilight's glow, a solemn fight.
Against the shadows creeping in,
To keep the light within, to win.

Stars observe this endless task,
In nature's glory, no need to ask.
A quiet vigil, strong and bright,
In heights so pure, a hopeful sight.

Eyes of the Sky

Azure giants watch from above,
Silent keepers of boundless love.
Through day's bright sun and night's soft pry,
In their gaze, all mysteries lie.

Skyward eyes of infinite lore,
Seeing oceans, mountains, and more.
Clouds like whispers in their domain,
Every storm just a fleeting strain.

Under their watch, life blooms and fades,
Seasons cycle in their charades.
Observing all with steady grace,
Eyes of the sky, an endless chase.

Forgotten Heights

In twilight's silent silver gleam,
When dreams ascend to unseen peaks,
Beyond the edges of the stream,
Lie secrets lofty silence speaks.

Whispers woven in the wind,
Echoes of the ancients' song,
Time loses what it could not find,
In heights forgotten, shadows long.

Summits touch a boundless sky,
Star-kissed brows, a dusky hue,
In stillness, silent mountains lie,
Guardians of the hidden view.

Vista of Vultures

Circling high in skies of grey,
An omen, watchful eyes that gleam,
On rugged cliffs they hold their sway,
Silent reapers in a dream.

Underneath their vast domain,
Shadows cast by wings of fate,
Life returns to dust again,
Cradled by the hands of weight.

Eternal guardians in flight,
Witnesses to nature's end,
Within their vista, day to night,
Cycles of the earth they tend.

Decayed Domain

Once proud structures now in dust,
Echoes of a time long gone,
Bones of iron turn to rust,
In this realm where shadows fawn.

Ghosts of grandeur linger still,
In the quiet of the night,
Haunting ruins on a hill,
With memories distant, out of sight.

Broken stones and whispers low,
Mark the end of glory's reign,
In this place where legends go,
A kingdom lost, decayed domain.

Sentinel of Silence

In the stillness of the dawn,
A lone watchman takes his place,
Half in shadow, half withdrawn,
Stoic figure with no face.

Guarding secrets of the night,
Silent as the falling dew,
Eyes that pierce the greatest light,
Keeper of the ancient true.

Time's companion, ever still,
Witness to both joy and strife,
In the silence of the hill,
Sentinel who watches life.

Perch of Fate

Upon the branch of destiny,
A bird alights in twilight's glow.
Beyond the veil of what shall be,
Whispers of fate begin to flow.

The stars align in secret dance,
Crafting paths we cannot see.
In shadows cast, a silent chance,
Guides the bird, and guides me.

The wind sings songs of days gone by,
Remnants of hope, of dreams fulfilled.
In every breath, a gentle sigh,
As time stands still, the air is stilled.

Eyes that gleam with ancient lore,
Gaze into the heart of night.
And though the future's still unsure,
The soul soars free, takes flight.

Watcher in the Winds

High above the earthly scape,
A watcher soars on wings of pride,
In currents cold, in air escapes,
Where endless dreams and hopes reside.

Whispered secrets ride the breeze,
Angelic hymns from realms unknown.
Below, the world rests at ease,
While in the sky, the winds have grown.

Eyes that pierce the darkened shroud,
Bear witness to the dawn's first light.
Silent, stoic, never loud,
Guardian of the stars so bright.

Bound to no terrestrial tether,
In ethereal grace, it swoops and glides,
Ever watchful, in stormy weather,
A faithful sentinel in the tides.

Sky's Custodian

Majestic in the azure sea,
A custodian of skies prevails.
Guarding realms of clouds so free,
Where serenade of wind unveils.

With wings like whispered lullabies,
It charts a course through sunlit beams.
Through tempest roars and calmest sighs,
Keeper of celestial dreams.

In every feather, wisdom's trace,
Reflections of eternal skies.
In boundless, high, ethereal space,
It sails where only truth lies.

Ageless eyes that see the all,
The changing tides of night and day.
In service to the sky's great call,
Its boundless spirit finds its way.

Grim Soarer

In the twilight's chilling hue,
A figure soars on wings of fate.
Grim and silent, cutting through,
The veil of dusk, a somber state.

Shadows drape its slender form,
As whispers pierce the evening's breath.
In the heart of every storm,
A testament to life and death.

With eyes that gleam like ancient steel,
It surveys lands both far and near.
Harbinger of truths concealed,
Bearer of the silent fear.

Yet in its grim and ghostly flight,
There lies a beauty dark, profound.
For in the depths of endless night,
A sense of peace, at last, is found.

Scavenger's Sky

In the rustle of wings above the moor,
Crows dance, their shadows whispering lore.
The sky an endless sheet of grey,
Where scavengers trace their autumn ballet.

They circle high, on currents wide,
In search of secrets the earth won't hide.
Each feather a brushstroke on canvas vast,
Sketching tales of future and past.

The sun dips low, an ember lain,
Against the quilted clouds of rain.
In twilight's grasp, the hunters soar,
Painting twilight myths forevermore.

City lights loom, distant, bare,
As night conceals their aerial affair.
Stars sprinkle down in fragments sly,
To join the dance in a scavenger's sky.

Echo in the Air

A whisper leaps from mountain high,
To kiss the vale and drift the sky.
An echo in the air it turns,
In endless loops it twists and yearns.

The wind, a herald of lost refrain,
Carries voices, ease and pain.
It tells of love and battles won,
Of rivers' courses, duty done.

Among the leaves, it weaves its song,
A chorus fleeting, never long.
In half-lit dusk, in break of dawn,
An echo's life is here then gone.

In quiet moments, pause to hear
The stories whispered, far and near.
For echoes carve with gentle care,
Their transient verses, lost in air.

Feathers and Finality

At twilight's edge, the feathers fall,
Beneath the silent forest's call.
Each plume a tale of quests pursued,
And final flights in solitude.

The moonlight glints on wings at rest,
In nests where dreams and fate digest.
The finality of one last flight,
Embraced by shadows of the night.

With whispered wind, the feathers drift,
In unseen currents, voices lift.
From branch to ground, the silent song,
Of journeys brief and nights so long.

Feathers mark what time can't heal,
Each down a memory, harsh or real.
In quiet groves where echoes meet,
Finality wraps the flights complete.

Vaulted Vistas

Gaze where heaven and earth align,
In vaulted vistas, scenes divine.
Peaks touch clouds of marshmallow dreams,
We're lost in nature's laced extremes.

The valleys dip with verdant grace,
As rivers carve their endless race.
Each fold in land, a tale untold,
A masterpiece of green and gold.

Horizons stretch in whispered hues,
With skies that shift in sunset blues.
In twilight's amber, shadows trace,
The quiet dance of day's embrace.

Say a prayer in fields of light,
Where day meets dusk and love takes flight.
In vaulted vistas, take your stand,
With dreams imprinted on the land.

Gyres of Fate

In circles, life and dreams, they spin,
Emerging from the depths within.
A story carved by unseen hands,
Spirals traced in shifting sands.

From dawn's first light to dark's embrace,
The gyres of fate, we dare to face.
Clockwork whispers, shadows loom,
Guiding us through time's ballroom.

Each choice, a ripple in the stream,
Each moment, part of some vast scheme.
In currents deep, we find our way,
In gyres of fate, we dance and sway.

Doom of the Downed

Beneath, where light does fail to seep,
In caverns dark and waters deep,
Lies the doom of those who fall,
Echoing in an endless call.

With shadows thick and whispers cold,
The tales of sorrow often told,
In the depths where hope is drowned,
Rest the souls forever bound.

Yet in the dark, a spark remains,
A silent plea, a call for change.
For even in the deepest night,
The heart yearns for a ray of light.

Skyward Seeker

Eyes lifted to the vast expanse,
On wings of dreams, the heart's romance.
A world below in fleeting glances,
Above, the sky invites our dances.

In azure seas where clouds do sail,
Our spirits soar, our hopes prevail.
From peaks of mountains to the stars,
We reach beyond, despite the scars.

With every leap, our doubts grow small,
In every rise, we stand more tall.
Skyward, ever seeking, free,
Boundless as eternity.

Eyes on Eternity

Gaze fixed upon the endless span,
Where time and space entwine their plan.
Eternity in silent sweep,
Awakens stars from cosmic sleep.

In moments vast, the soul's embrace,
Through boundless night, we seek our place.
Evolving, ever, dreams unfold,
In whispers of the tales untold.

Eyes on eternity, we stride,
Through realms of thought, with hearts as guide.
In every heartbeat, echoes blend,
A timeless journey, without end.

Confluence of Currents

Rivers merge in ancient dance,
Currents kiss in tidal trance,
Where the waters sing and prance,
Harmony in every glance.

Mountains weep their snowy springs,
Echoes soar on gulls' white wings,
Nature's song in ripple rings,
Whispers of the world it brings.

Bridges span the liquid flows,
Human hands where nature grows,
History within it shows,
Stories written as it goes.

Fish in schools, a flashing gleam,
Birds above the mirrored stream,
Life and water weave a dream,
Joining forces in a theme.

Stone and shell on riverbed,
Pathways where the creatures tread,
Silent tales of living thread,
In their confluence, we are led.

Above the Carrion

Vultures circle in the sky,
Painted wings, a dark ally,
Silent oaths, they prophesy,
On the breezes, low and high.

Bones and feathers mark the ground,
Echoes of the fallen sound,
In the circle, life is found,
Nature's dance is all around.

Eyes that pierce the earthly veil,
Messages in wing and tale,
In the silence, we prevail,
Life continues to exhale.

Beasts below and birds above,
Witness to the ebb of love,
In their shadows, whispers of
Ancient truths we're part of.

Endings here are not the end,
In decay, new lives extend,
Harmony, our hearts comprehend,
In the skies the seekers send.

Shadows on the Sand

Mirrors of the setting sun,
Reflecting gold and silver spun,
Where the waves and earth are one,
Shadows whispered, never done.

Footprints left and then erased,
By the sea's eternally paced,
Time in grains, a memory traced,
Silent echoes interlaced.

Dunes and cliffs in solemn guard,
Secrets kept and yet unmarred,
Life is fleeting, moments starred,
Nature's poem, softly scarred.

Whispers in the twilight sighed,
In the shoreline, softly tied,
Where the shadows long abide,
And in silence, truths confide.

Night descends with velvet hand,
Stars above and shadows planned,
Stories written on the sand,
Eternal tales of sea and land.

Twilight's Surveyor

In the twilight, shadows grow,
Silent watchers' gleaning glow,
Surveyor of both high and low,
Moonlit paths the stars bestow.

Sky in hues of dusk and dawn,
Every breath a fleeting fawn,
Past and future gently drawn,
Moments spun on nature's lawn.

Eyes that see beyond our veil,
Guide the journey, set the sail,
In the dusk where whispers trail,
Every heartbeat tells a tale.

Contours faint in silver sheen,
Dreams and echoes intervene,
In the night where sights are seen,
Shadows mark what we have been.

Twilight's surveyor, ancient knower,
Keeper of the times and slower,
In their watch, the moments lower,
Ever present, ever sower.

The Great Hover

In skies where dreams take flight,
A feather's gentle drift,
Gliding through the night,
In currents, spirits lift.

Ephemeral whispers sing,
Across the moonlit sea,
The Great Hover's wing,
Marks endless liberty.

Each breath a silent dance,
In vast celestial dome,
Boundless, souls advance,
In ether's endless home.

No anchor, chain, or tie,
Can halt the boundless sweep;
In twilight's quiet sigh,
We float through cosmic deep.

Gaze of the Heights

From mountaintop's embrace,
A world unveiled below,
In each cloud's gentle trace,
The winds of wonder blow.

The crest, a throne of skies,
Where eagles carve their path,
In sunlit peaks that rise,
To heavens' whispered wrath.

Gaze of the heights so pure,
A sentinel of dreams,
In valleys' green allure,
The river's silver streams.

Ascend through trails untold,
To realms where stars ignite,
In silent moments bold,
We claim the endless night.

Eternal Circulator

Through corridors of time,
A ceaseless, rhythmic beat,
Eternal circulator's rhyme,
In heart's unyielding heat.

The seasons' endless waltz,
A mirror to our days,
In nature's gentle pulse,
Life's cyclic, timeless phase.

In rivers' flowing thread,
And winds that never rest,
The cosmic round is led,
By fate's unerring quest.

A path with no defined end,
A journey ever new,
In cycles we transcend,
Eternal, we and you.

Grim Contour

In shadows' somber trace,
The grim contour takes form,
A silhouette's embrace,
In twilight's ghostly storm.

Through mists of quiet fear,
Where whispers linger still,
Each line a stark frontier,
Of fate's unyielding will.

The night's encroaching hand,
Draws figures in the gloom,
With silent, sure command,
Each shadow finds its room.

In darkened corners lie,
The shapes of what has been,
Grim contours never die,
In haunting, veiled sheen.

Echoes in the Breeze

Whispers through the ancient trees,
Silent murmurs, soft and free,
Nature's voice in gentle pleas,
Carried on the calmest sea.

Leaves that dance in twilight's glow,
Echoes from the past they know,
Speak of tales from long ago,
In a language soft and slow.

Shadows play where light once streamed,
In the meadows of our dreams,
Memories of moments gleamed,
In the echoes of the breeze.

Silent harmonies take flight,
Winged upon the cloak of night,
Fading into morning light,
Lost within the day's new sight.

Touch the whispers, hear their call,
Answer softly, one and all,
Feel their presence gently fall,
Echoes in the breeze enthrall.

Silent Sentinels

Guardians of secrets old,
Silent sentinels, calm and bold,
Stories of the woods they hold,
In their hearts of timeless gold.

Standing through the storms' embrace,
Winds that shift and skies which chase,
They remain in steadfast grace,
Keeper of the sacred space.

Bark of wisdom, roots of might,
Silent in the darkest night,
They observe the stars' bright light,
Knowing each one's ancient flight.

Time may pass and seasons turn,
Still, their silent watch will burn,
Through the years, they will discern,
Lessons that the world must learn.

Honor those who stand in peace,
From their watch will never cease,
In their presence, find release,
Silent sentinels' gentle ease.

Windswept Watcher

Perched upon a craggy height,
Eyes that pierce the coming night,
Watcher of the winds' swift flight,
Guardian in fading light.

Feathers ruffle in the breeze,
Echoes of the winds that tease,
Boundless sky and endless seas,
In the wings of timeless ease.

Through the valleys, over plains,
Soaring where the spirit reigns,
Free from all of life's remains,
Casting shadows with no chains.

Mysteries within its gaze,
Unraveled in the twilight haze,
Ancient rites of bygone days,
Witnessed in the sunset's blaze.

Higher still it climbs and soars,
Past the earthly bars and doors,
Windswept watcher, spirit roars,
Till the ending time restores.

Soaring Shadows

On the mountains high they glide,
Shadows soaring, far and wide,
In their flight, the day they bide,
Merging with the evening tide.

Wings outstretched to catch the glow,
Of the sun as it sinks low,
In their path, the winds will flow,
Carrying tales of long ago.

Through the skies they weave and sway,
Silent guardians of the day,
Marking paths that lead away,
To where the night and dreams convey.

Silhouettes against the sky,
Tracing patterns you can't deny,
Mysteries that seem to fly,
Lingering, as time goes by.

Soaring shadows, bold and free,
In their grace, we too can see,
Echoes of eternity,
In the dance of sky and sea.

Carrion Watcher

Upon the branch a shadow waits,
Eyes like embers in the night.
Wings black as forgotten fates,
Silent harbinger, keeper of blight.

Circling high and falling slow,
Patient vulture bears no dread.
Where life's pulse no longer flows,
It seeks the silent, still, and dead.

In twilight's waning, unseen quest,
Feathers rustle, whispers weave.
It finds its solace in the rest,
Of what we mourn and what we grieve.

The world turns on, uncaring clock,
Time erodes both stone and scar.
Watch the watcher, cold as rock,
Sentinel from long afar.

Beneath its gaze, earth reclaims,
All that once held breath and fire.
Circle, carrion watcher, flames,
Fade into your endless pyre.

Grace in Decay

Golden leaves in autumn's grasp,
Fall in silent, amber rain.
Beauty held in time's slow clasp,
Whispered tales of joy and pain.

Roses wither, petals drift,
In the dance of life's soft wane.
In decay, they give a gift,
Grace that blossoms not in vain.

Crumbling walls with ivy crowned,
Ruins wear their age with pride.
Echoes of the past resound,
Stories in their stones reside.

Moss on gravestones, velvet green,
Softens granite's stark decree.
In the fading, life is seen,
Hope within the entropy.

For in ending, there's a rebirth,
Cycles spinning round and round.
From the ashes of the earth,
Grace in decay can be found.

Feathers and Ash

Like smoke among the starless skies,
Shoals of feathers dark and bright.
Burnt in fire, born to rise,
From ash, they seek the light.

In the quiet, wings unfold,
Ephemeral, yet bold they soar.
Through tempests fierce and bitter cold,
They chase the dreams they bore.

Flames have whispered secrets lost,
Of battles fought within the heart.
Where feathers meet with ashes tossed,
And scarred souls find their start.

In the dusk where shadows creep,
And embers glow with fading breath,
Feathers whisper songs of sleep,
And dance upon the edge of death.

In the dawn, the phoenix calls,
Through realms where spirits clash.
Reborn anew, defying falls,
In realms of feathers and ash.

Silent Glide

Across the sky in twilight's hug,
An owl glides on silent wings.
Night's embrace, a velvet rug,
In silence, the soft voice sings.

Moon's soft gaze in stars' embrace,
Guides the flight of spectral guide.
In the stillness, find their grace,
Wild and free in silent glide.

Through the forest, shadows play,
As whispers of the wind entwine.
In the night's soft, silent sway,
Mystery and magic combine.

Eyes that pierce the darkest veil,
Glimmer with a knowing light.
In their glide, a hidden trail,
Leads through the secrets of the night.

Embrace the night, and in its hide,
Find the peace, calm and wide.
With the owl in moonlit tide,
Set your soul in silent glide.

Rider of the Thermals

On wings that carve the sky's embrace,
Rider of the thermals, without a trace,
You glide where only few have tread,
Through boundless blue, your spirit fed.

Amidst the clouds, you find your path,
Defying gravity's quiet wrath,
A dance of freedom, wild and wide,
With nature as your faithful guide.

Each spiral up, a silent prayer,
To winds that whisper, skies that care,
And sunbeams kiss your feathered flight,
A guardian of the morning light.

Mountains bow and valleys rise,
Beneath your watchful, piercing eyes,
A monarch of the endless air,
Unfettered, free from earthly care.

So spread your wings, oh sovereign bird,
For in your flight, a truth is heard,
That life, like wind, is best embraced,
In soaring freedom, fierce and chased.

Above Life's End

In twilight's gentle, fading hue,
Above life's end, a vision true,
Souls are lifted to the sky,
Where eternal whispers softly lie.

No chains of time, no bounds of space,
In this serene and sacred place,
Where every tear and sorrow mend,
Above life's end, where paths transcend.

The stars become a soothing guide,
For spirits seeking a new tide,
Beyond the veil, a calm begins,
A universe where love now wins.

The earth below, a distant past,
Its memories forever cast,
Yet in the heavens, wide and vast,
Souls find peace and home at last.

In timeless tapestries, they weave,
Stories that our hearts believe,
That even death's most silent bend,
Leads to freedom without end.

Eclipse in Feathers

When shadows cloak the midday sun,
An eclipse in feathers has begun,
With wings outstretched in solemn grace,
A veil descends upon the space.

A raven's call, so dark and clear,
Echoes secrets we hold dear,
Night invades the sunny skies,
In feathers black, a world disguised.

The forest stills, the creatures halt,
As night and day suspend their waltz,
A cosmic dance that few have seen,
In twilight's grip, a midnight sheen.

The sun will shine, but not for now,
As shadows whisper through the bough,
In wings of black, their stories meld,
An eclipse in feathers - power held.

Yet soon the light, it will return,
And daylight from the dark will learn,
That in the shadows, we too find,
A touch of grace, both intertwined.

Silent Circles

In silent circles, whispers flow,
Where rivers of the ages go,
Beneath the stars, their journeys wind,
In cosmic dance, threads they bind.

The moon will cast her silver veil,
Upon the seas, the ships set sail,
Time and tide in eerie tune,
Beneath the gaze of sun and moon.

Life's cycles traced in sand and stone,
In silent circles, wisdom's sown,
Nature's echo, pure and deep,
In hallowed moments, shadows keep.

From birth to death, each step we trace,
In silent circles, endless grace,
The laughter, tears, the love, the pain,
All converge in life's refrain.

Thus round we go in timeless drift,
Where moments meet and spirits lift,
In silent circles, we belong,
A never-ending, ancient song.

Aether's Scavenger

Through lofty clouds the drifter roams,
Collecting whispers, forgotten homes.
In spectral winds, his fingers graze,
The echoes lost in twilight's haze.

Stars glean secrets of ages past,
In silence vast, his shadows cast.
Ephemeral threads in darkness weave,
A thousand stories he does conceive.

With moonlit gauntlets, treasures find,
In realms unseen, within the mind.
From dusk till dawn, his quest persists,
Among the constellations' mists.

No map to guide, no compass drawn,
He dances with the break of dawn.
Aether's scavenger, a phantom's plight,
Eternally tethered to the night.

In cosmic tides, his fate aligns,
The wanderer of astral signs.
His silent journey, ever fair,
In solemn vigil through the air.

Night's Custodian

When day departs and shadows creep,
A guardian wakes from timeless sleep.
Veiled in darkness, softly tread,
To guard the dreams where fears are fed.

Beneath the eaves where secrets lie,
He watches with a vigilant eye.
With cloak of stars and whispered plea,
He shepherds through night's mystery.

The luna's light his lantern glows,
Through haunted dusk his presence flows.
Sleepless sentinel, calm and still,
His steady watch a tranquil thrill.

No dawn can break his solemn vow,
In twilight's web, his silent bow.
A custodian of sable wynds,
He navigates where dream entwines.

With tender grace he holds the doors,
Of every night, to evermore.
In shadows deep, his heart stays true,
Until at last, the sky turns blue.

Silent Reclaimer

In forests thick where silence reigns,
A figure moves through ancient veins.
Each step a whisper, soft and light,
Collecting shadows from the night.

The fallen leaves his path betray,
Yet softly does he wind his way.
With hand on heart, he mends the scar,
Of time's relentless, lingering mar.

He takes the whispers of the past,
And breathes them into futures vast.
The echoes fade, yet not in vain,
Restored by him, through dusk and rain.

In ruins where old dreams reside,
He walks, a ghost, as winds subside.
The silent reclaimer, unseen, unfound,
He heals the earth without a sound.

By morning light, his work concealed,
The scars of time and pain are healed.
A guardian of dreams and lore,
Who walks the world forevermore.

Soul's Gatekeeper

At twilight's end where two paths meet,
He stands with silence at his feet.
In eyes of fire, a wisdom deep,
He guards the gates where spirits sleep.

With solemn gaze, he weighs the heart,
In realms where mortal and stars part.
Through ether's veil his whispers weave,
Deciding those who may believe.

He holds the key to light and dark,
To every soul, a glowing spark.
With gentle hand or iron fist,
Each destiny is shaped and kissed.

No mortal knows the path he treads,
Between the living and the dead.
The soul's gatekeeper, firm and true,
Guides mysteries to mornings new.

In endless night, his watch remains,
Through joy and sorrow, loss and gains.
Akeeper of the endless door,
He guards the realms forevermore.

Talon and Bones

In the forest deep, where shadows dance,
Talon sharp, a bird seeks chance.
Bones beneath the ancient oak,
Whisper secrets, softly spoke.

Feathers dark as twilight's shroud,
Pierce the stillness, proud and loud.
Memories lost in earthen grave,
Echoes of the brave and grave.

Underneath the silent moon,
Nature croons her timeless tune.
Cycles spin and fade away,
Day to night and night to day.

Talon hunts, a life to claim,
Bones remain, an endless name.
In this realm, both fierce and mild,
Lives are but a fleeting wild.

In the end, we're all the same,
Talon's grip or bone's acclaim.
Life and death in nature's plan,
The timeless tale of beast and man.

Threshold of Silence

At twilight's edge, a whisper born,
On lips of dusk, the day is worn.
Steps uncertain, shadows grow,
To cross the threshold, worlds below.

Silence gathers, breath held firm,
Moments linger, thoughts affirm.
Dreams once spoken, now retreat,
In silence find, the heartbeat's beat.

Against the veil of night so still,
A wave of calm, a soothing thrill.
Stars above like watchers keen,
Guard the passage, unseen, serene.

Voices past, they softly call,
In the quiet, hear them all.
Echoes weave a tender thread,
Guiding souls where angels tread.

Threshold crossed, the silent sphere,
Worries fade and night is clear.
In the stillness, truth revealed,
Peace and beauty, both concealed.

Wings Over Desolation

In the barren waste, where silence speaks,
Wings take flight over desolate peaks.
Eagles soar on thermal streams,
Guiding hearts with whispered dreams.

Dust and bone beneath the sky,
Life persists, though waters dry.
Desolation's harsh embrace,
Yet still the wings, with hope, do trace.

Midday sun, a blistered glare,
Scorched earth cries, yet eagles dare.
Through the vast and empty space,
They find a path, a saving grace.

Wings spread wide in boundless flight,
Chasing shadows through the night.
Beacons of a world reborn,
In their flight, a new dawn sworn.

Hope alight on feathered wing,
Desolation's dirge they sing.
Life must fight and life must strain,
But in the wings, a world regained.

Keeper of the Departed

In the twilight's gentle fold,
Lies a keeper, wise and old.
Guarding souls of those who've flown,
To realms unseen, the spirits' home.

Veils of mist and shadows blend,
Where dreams and memories transcend.
Whispers soft in twilight's shroud,
Echoes speak from past endowed.

Lanterns dim and candles fade,
Keeper walks through evening's shade.
Guiding lights for lost to see,
Paths to traverse, wild and free.

Murmurs of the autumn leaves,
Tell of last breath, hearts that grieve.
Yet in keeper's gentle care,
Hope resides, a love laid bare.

Bound by duty, fate's own thread,
Keeper watches, honors dead.
In the silence, secrets keep,
Guarding peace as shadows sleep.

Doom's Flightpath

In shadows deep, the night does creep,
A silent wail through skies so steep.
Stars shiver, in their powdered light,
As doom takes wings on its flightpath bright.

With whispers cold, it charts its course,
Through realms where dreams are torn by force.
A harbinger of fate unknown,
In midnight's grip, all seeds are sown.

No mortal eye can grasp its stride,
For doom knows paths where fears reside.
A journey through the heart of night,
Where spirits fade in silent sight.

Against the gale, it boldly flies,
Unveiling secrets of the skies.
Destiny in talons tight,
It crafts its tale in endless flight.

Through veils of time, it weaves and grows,
As legends whisper, truth bestows.
Doom's flightpath, a haunting trace,
Etched forever in cosmic grace.

Wings Above Dust

In fields where silence keeps its trust,
A whisper stirs above the dust.
Through barren lands, a feathered hush,
With wings that gleam in twilight's blush.

Beyond the grasp of earthly chain,
They soar where only dreams remain.
In hues of dawn and twilight's glow,
A dance of grace above below.

Where weary hearts to wonder cling,
And heavy souls lift to spring.
Their flight a promise in the skies,
Freedom found where vision lies.

Above the storm, beyond the ire,
They rise on currents of desire.
A symphony of breath and sky,
In whispered winds, they softly fly.

The dust below, a realm of chains,
Yet here, in air, no sorrow reigns.
With every beat, a story spun,
Of wings that rise 'til day is done.

The Heiress of Ashes

In the wake of fire's embrace,
She rises, clad in ash and grace.
From ruins wrought by time and flame,
The heiress holds a silent claim.

Her throne, a pyre of dreams once bright,
Now shadows dance in pale moonlight.
Embers whisper tales of old,
Of kingdoms lost and hearts grown cold.

Eyes of flame and breath of heat,
She walks where worlds and echoes meet.
In ashes, new foundations brew,
A legacy forged, a future's view.

Through desolation, hope ignites,
A spark that shatters endless nights.
The heiress of the ashes stands,
With power held in tender hands.

From cinders, life begins anew,
A cycle born in burnt-out view.
The past consumed, the future burns,
In ashen fields, the world turns.

Twilight's Talon

When day concedes to twilight's claim,
A talon grips the edge of flame.
With shadows deep and skies alight,
It carves a path through coming night.

The sun retreats, its final sigh,
As stars awaken, filling sky.
In twilight's grip, the talon's might,
Unveiling secrets of the night.

Through veiled realms of dusk it flies,
Where mortal dreams and truth arise.
In silent sweep of evening's wing,
A symphony of night to sing.

With strength that shatters light's domain,
It heralds night's profound refrain.
In twilight's breath, the worlds align,
A passage through the great divine.

A talon sharp, a guide through dark,
Imprints of stars its fleeting mark.
In twilight's grasp, all fears are gone,
As night and dreams embrace the dawn.

Sentry of the Abyss

In shadows deep where monsters crawl,
A sentry stands, observing all.
Eyes that pierce the darkest night,
In the abyss, devoid of light.

Through eerie mists and silence cold,
Ancient stories left untold.
Keeper of the void's embrace,
Guarding secrets, lost in space.

Beneath the waves of time's dread tide,
Echoes of the fallen bide.
The sentry's watch, eternal claim,
In abyssal dark, unnamed.

From hollow depths where whispers soar,
Guarding what came long before.
Silent watch in endless black,
No return, no turning back.

Eternal vigil, lone and stark,
In the abyss, no end, no spark.
A silent sentinel in murky gloom,
Guarding an unending tomb.

Heaven's Carrion

Beneath the sky's cerulean tears,
In heaven's lofty, hallowed spheres.
Carrion birds in flight, they roam,
Searching for a spectral home.

With wings of shadow, eyes so keen,
They haunt the realms of those unseen.
Devouring memories of yore,
On heavenly heights, they soar.

Ethereal winds that whisper low,
Carry secrets none can know.
Beacons of the past they follow,
In the sky, both fierce and hollow.

Feathers drift down like plumes of night,
In the just dawn's waking light.
Hunters of a timeless quest,
In heaven's expanse, they never rest.

Skyward sentinels of decay,
Through celestial ash, they flay.
Heaven's carrion, dark circles wheel,
In a dance both cold and real.

Perished Lands Below

Beneath the earth where shadows dwell,
Lies a world, a sunken shell.
Perished lands of silent woe,
Hidden secrets deep below.

Ashen fields and withered trees,
Silent graves, ghostly pleas.
Echoes of the lives once bright,
Now succumbed to endless night.

Time has stopped in this forlorn place,
Leaving but a haunted trace.
In the silence, shadows grow,
Of the perished lands below.

Whispers carried on the breeze,
Of ancient sorrow, lost decrees.
What was gold now turned to dust,
Beneath the ground, decay and rust.

Through twilight's veil and sinking gloom,
Lies beneath a quiet tomb.
Perished lands where spirits cry,
In eternal by and by.

Circling Specter

A phantom cloaked in silver mist,
Circling where the shadows twist.
A specter's waltz in moonlit glow,
Silent as the falling snow.

Ethereal dance on midnight breeze,
Haunting whispers through the trees.
Round and round in endless flight,
A ghostly figure, pale and light.

Eyes that gleam like distant stars,
Bound by neither life nor bars.
Spectral form in timeless plight,
Circles through the endless night.

Ancient stories in its wake,
Forsaken dreams it cannot shake.
Veil of night, its cursed tether,
Binding ghost and shadow together.

Through the night and through the gloom,
Silently it weaves its loom.
A circling specter, lost in time,
Eternally in mime sublime.

Wings of the Scavenger

Against the wind, in silent grace,
It soars in search of life's embrace.
A watchful eye, a keen desire,
To find what falls, to never tire.

In barren lands and fields of grey,
It marks the end of life's brief play.
A silent witness to decay,
Yet brings forth balance day by day.

On vast horizons, black as night,
It spreads its wings, a harbinger's flight.
With patience born of ancient lore,
It waits, and life it shall restore.

Feathers sleek and eyes that gleam,
A guardian of the night's dark dream.
Not feared nor loved, but oft ignored,
Still part of tales of life restored.

In every gust and whispering breeze,
It finds its path with practiced ease.
Wings of the scavenger, shadows cast,
Reminders of a future past.

Circling Above

High above the world below,
It circles wide in rhythmic flow.
A dance with air, a silent prayer,
To find the fate that's hidden there.

Eyes sharp as eagles, keen with light,
It marks the day, it marks the night.
An endless wheel of life and death,
In every wing beat, in every breath.

From dawn till dusk in skies so blue,
It traces life's path true to true.
No sound or song it needs to play,
A guardian for the end of day.

In lofty heights it makes its home,
In constant travel it does roam.
A silent partner to the Earth,
To mark each ending, each new birth.

Above the storms, above the strife,
It holds the thread of fragile life.
Circling above, it seeks and finds,
The echoes of the fate that binds.

Sentry of the Skies

With feathers dark and eyes that gleam,
It watches o'er the land and stream.
A sentry poised in silent flight,
A keeper of the day and night.

It glides on currents high and true,
Its vision pierces through the blue.
A guardian of the skies so vast,
It holds the memory of the past.

In every gust, in every gale,
It reads the stories each wind tells.
A sentry bound by ancient call,
To witness rise, to witness fall.

In shadows deep and sunlight bright,
It keeps its vigil, day to night.
An everlasting sight to see,
A symbol of what is, what'll be.

As long as skies remain so wide,
Its wings will span from side to side.
A sentry of the skies it flies,
With endless stories in its eyes.

Watcher of the Wastes

In desolation, barren place,
It finds its purpose, finds its grace.
A watcher of the wastes it flies,
With ancient wisdom in its eyes.

Through endless dunes and dry, cracked earth,
It seeks the cycle of rebirth.
Amidst the silence, harsh and still,
It spreads its wings, it finds its fill.

Above the wastelands, stark and cold,
It searches for the tales untold.
A witness to the barren plains,
It soars through winds and desert rains.

In emptiness, it finds its role,
It guards the secrets, guards each soul.
A lonely vigil in the sands,
A keeper of these vast, dry lands.

As long as deserts stretch and sway,
It holds its watch both night and day.
A watcher of the wastes, it flies,
With endless questions in its eyes.

Keeper of Carrion

In shadows deep where silence sighs,
The keeper dwells with unseen eyes.
Among the bones laid bare to rest,
A guardian of the solemn crest.

No mourner's tears, no grieving cries,
Just whispers where the dark bird flies.
So still the night, a breathless loom,
Weaving tales of the tomb.

Echoes fade in the haunted glen,
The past retreats time and again.
Silent watch and sleepless dreams,
Where the moon coldly beams.

The keeper's throne is solitude,
Among the stones, the shadows brood.
By nature's laws, in duty bound,
In silence, secrets are found.

Eternal vigil in the hushed abyss,
A keeper of what time dismiss.
Yet in the quiet, there's a song,
The keeper of carrion carries on.

Apex of Stillness

Upon the crest of twilight's peak,
Where silence speaks, but none shall speak.
There lies the realm where stillness dreams,
Of calming waves and endless streams.

The world slows down in hushed delight,
As shadows blend with fading light.
The stars appear, an ethereal seam,
Stitched in the fabric of a dream.

No wind disturbs the tranquil air,
The breath of night is pure and rare.
A moment bathed in sacred grace,
A tender touch on nature's face.

Here, whispers quiet as they form,
A solace found within the storm.
The chaos bows to night's embrace,
At the apex of stillness, peace has a place.

In this silence, hearts can mend,
The rush of life comes to an end.
For here, we find the soul's true call,
Within the stillness, we feel all.

Whispers on the Wind

Across the vast and open plain,
There whispers secrets wrapped in rain.
A murmur soft through fields does wend,
The stories told by wind, my friend.

In gusts and breezes, voices weave,
Tales of those who used to cleave.
Fragile dreams and broken hearts,
Scattered wide in wind-blown parts.

Mountains echo long-lost songs,
A soothing call where one belongs.
In every gale and sweet refrain,
Lives the dance of joy and pain.

The whispers hold a truth so rare,
A lover's sigh, a prayer, a dare.
In nature's breath, we're all entwined,
By whispers carried on the wind.

So, listen closely, heart to sky,
Hear the past and present fly.
In whispers, tales will never end,
Our souls aloft, the wind's best friend.

Oracle of Endings

In twilight's gleam, near dusk's rebirth,
An oracle walks the edge of earth.
With eyes that pierce the veils of fate,
He whispers what the stars create.

Behind the shroud of darkened skies,
He sees the truth where silence lies.
Endings woven in the skein,
Of destiny's unfurling chain.

Each breath he takes, a prophecy,
An echo of what is to be.
For when the day surrenders light,
The oracle brings forth the night.

Guided by a voiceless song,
He knows that endings all belong.
To the cycle, birth to end,
Time the secret he'll defend.

And so, with gentle, knowing hand,
He writes the final, silent strand.
The oracle of endings blends,
Beginnings with the way life bends.

Aerial Harbinger

High above in evening's grace,
Wings of silver slice the sky,
Through the clouds in solemn chase,
Silent as the night looms nigh.

Herald of a hidden fate,
Messenger of dawn's first light,
Shadows fall as dark grows late,
Guiding through the endless night.

Whispers carried on the breeze,
Secrets of the earth below,
Echoes of the ancient seas,
Mysteries that ever flow.

In the twilight's gentle glow,
Where the stars begin to peek,
The aerial harbinger will show,
Paths that only dreamers seek.

Bones Under Beak

In the stillness of the grave,
Where the whispers cease to speak,
Lies a secret only brave,
Hidden bones beneath the beak.

Feathers cloak a tale untold,
Of a past that lingers near,
In the earth both dark and cold,
Silent cries no one can hear.

With each flight above the land,
Shadows dance and memories wake,
Nature's hand in solemn band,
Bones below will seldom break.

Life and death in mystic play,
Cycle spun in endless streak,
In the night and through the day,
Bones await beneath the beak.

Talon in the Twilight

As the dusk begins to fall,
Shifting hues in twilight's veil,
Talon sharp and standing tall,
Stalks where shadows softly pale.

Hunter of the ev'ning dusk,
Silent glide through fading light,
In the air a gentle musk,
Ancient ritual takes flight.

Eyes that pierce the darkened sky,
Eons old, a timeless sight,
Catch the prey though winds blow high,
Talon grips with fearsome might.

In the twilight's fleeting grace,
Nature's dance of life and strife,
Talon in the secret place,
Wields the balance, holds the life.

Veil of Viscera

Beneath the moon's ghostly beam,
In the forest's tangled weave,
Lies a realm of silent dream,
Where the night and shadows cleave.

Through the darkened branches sway,
Whispers of the unseen past,
Blood-soaked ground where spirits play,
Veil of viscera is cast.

Secrets of the ages lost,
In the shroud of ev'ning mist,
Nature claims at any cost,
Mystery and death persist.

In the heart of shadows deep,
Where the light and life inter,
Silent guardians keep their keep,
Veiled in visceral whisper.

High Altitude Perspective

Above the clouds we drift and sweep,
Where mountains kiss the sky so steep.
From vistas wide, the world looks grand,
A realm untouched by human hand.

The air is cold, but views ignite,
With colors bold, and sun's bright light.
Silent whispers of the breeze,
Carry tales from ancient seas.

Eagle's flight and thunder's roar,
Nature's symphony to explore.
Valleys green and rivers twist,
Paint a portrait that none can list.

Stars at night, a diamond veil,
Echo the calm in this high trail.
Skies embrace the tranquil height,
Revealing life's pure, sacred sight.

From peaks so tall, the soul expands,
As life's complex web it understands.
Horizon broad, horizons freed,
In high altitude, find your creed.

Silent Soar

Wings outspread, in hush they glide,
Through twilight's gentle, velvet tide.
In silence deep as night descends,
A journey vast, where vision wends.

Stars above and earth below,
In tranquil dance, the moments flow.
Moonlit paths in open sky,
Where dreams and whispers softly lie.

Without a sound, their freedom speaks,
Of endless skies and mountain peaks.
An echo in the stillness born,
Of timeless flight from dusk till dawn.

In silver shadows, they embark,
A voyage through the mystic dark.
No words are needed, none are missed,
In this serene and silent tryst.

As dawn emerges, golden crowned,
Their silent soar remains unbound.
Reminding us, though times are loud,
Quiet strength is ever proud.

Eyes from the Emptiness

In the void where shadows veer,
Eyes watch close, yet bring no fear.
From the darkness, silent gaze,
Seeks the light of brighter days.

Hidden depths, a calm they show,
Tales untold in watchful flow.
Wisdom dwells in empty sight,
Vision clear through endless night.

Mysteries within the black,
In those eyes, no path nor track.
Yet they see the world unfold,
Stories vast and truths untold.

Through the depths where silence swells,
Eyes from emptiness retell.
Every scar and bright expanse,
Ciphers in their tranquil trance.

Look beyond the voided space,
See the world at its base.
Eyes that pierce the dark we fear,
Draw us towards what we hold dear.

Guardians of Decay

In forests deep where shadows cling,
Old trees stand, in silence sing.
Guardians of time's slow march,
As nature weaves her ancient arch.

Roots entwined 'neath the dying leaf,
A solemn vow in tones of grief.
Echoes of the life now past,
In their presence forever cast.

Fungi bloom where sunlight dies,
Martyrs in decay's disguise.
They whisper secrets, soft and low,
Of cycles through which lifeforce flows.

Crumbling bark and withered vein,
Tell tales of strength and noble pain.
These sentinels in twilight's fall,
Bear witness to the eternal call.

Guardians stand as life decays,
In silent watch through endless days.
From dust to soil, then arise,
Their ancient song forever ties.

Necropolis Guardian

In shadows deep, where silence reigns,
A figure stands with ancient chains.
Whispers of the lost souls sing,
Under the moon's pale, spectral ring.

Guarding gates of time-worn stone,
With vigilant eyes, forever alone.
A sentinel in this city of night,
Bound by duty, hidden from light.

Specters gather at twilight's call,
Honoring the guardian who watches all.
Ethereal winds through corridors sweep,
Comforting those in their eternal sleep.

Forgotten memories in obsidian keep,
Cloaked in secrets dense and deep.
This hallowed ground, he treads with care,
Protecting the tranquility hidden there.

Beneath the stars, in the cold of dusk,
He whispers stories etched in musk.
A necropolis beneath his feet,
Where silence and shadow quietly meet.

Harbinger of Ends

Upon a steed of midnight hue,
The harbinger rides through skies anew.
With cloak of dusk and eyes so cold,
Foretelling tales yet to unfold.

Stars shiver and the moon does hide,
As he brings forth the coming tide.
Echoes of the fated succumb,
To whispers of what's yet to come.

Worlds tremble at his silent stride,
With destinies by his side.
The end of times, an age retreating,
In his presence, hearts stop beating.

Ancient prophecies etched in stone,
He carries forth, clandestine and lone.
Each breath he takes, a life unwinds,
As mortals grasp at fleeting binds.

In twilight's glow, his path defined,
A bringer of the end of time.
He casts his gaze, the final call,
Embracing twilight's silent thrall.

Wrath in Stillness

Beneath the calm of midnight's shroud,
A brewing storm, so fiercely proud.
In silence lies a wrath contained,
With vengeance that cannot be tamed.

Mountains echo distant cries,
Of anger hidden in disguise.
Rivers quake beneath the ground,
In stillness where the rage is found.

Silent skies yet thunder speaks,
A promise of the havoc it seeks.
Nature's fury waits in sleep,
In shadows where the silence creeps.

Eyes that burn with quiet flame,
In stillness, wrath shall stake its claim.
Unleashed, it shakes the very earth,
Birthed in silence, given worth.

The calm before the tempest true,
A wrath in stillness, breaking through.
The quiet soon will be upturned,
As silent fury's power's earned.

Lifeless Horizons

Across the barren, windswept dunes,
The silence of a lost world looms.
A canvas of endless, empty sands,
Where time slips through forgotten hands.

The sun sets on a cold desert plain,
No signs of life, no drops of rain.
A horizon draped in somber hues,
Echoes the absence in lonely views.

Mountains stand like sentinels old,
Guarding stories yet untold.
Among the desolate, dry expanse,
Dreams of life in death's cruel dance.

Skies weep with stars, their tears unseen,
Over landscapes washed of green.
In the quiet, a whisper cries,
Of what once was beneath these skies.

Lifeless horizons stretch afar,
Beneath a pale and distant star.
A sepulcher of nature's grace,
Silent, still, an empty space.

Sable Wings

In twilight skies, they take to flight,
With feathers dipped in midnight's dye.
Through shadowed realms, foreboding sight,
Sable wings adorn the sky.

They whisper tales of ancient woes,
Of kingdoms fallen, lost to time.
On sable wings, the tempest blows,
Echoes fading like a chime.

In moonlit silence, dreams take wing,
Eclipsing sun with darkened grace.
On sable winds, the sirens sing,
For mortals to an unknown place.

Silent Glade

In the heart of the silent glade,
Where whispers of the forest blend.
Beneath the canopy, hearts wade,
In quietude that has no end.

The brook's soft murmur, gently flows,
Caressing stones with liquid grace.
In the silent glade, peace bestows,
A haven in this tranquil space.

The spirit of the woods, unseen,
In every leaf, it weaves its thread.
Within the glade, where hearts convene,
Their souls in nature's lull are fed.

Final Breeze

In autumn's wake, the final breeze,
Caresses leaves, now browned with age.
Whispers through the forest's trees,
Turn the ever-changing page.

It carries tales of summer's end,
Of warmth that yields to cooler nights.
In the final breeze, we mend,
Our hearts in nature's shifting sights.

A gentle kiss, a fleeting touch,
Reminds of time and life's swift flow.
In the final breeze, we clutch,
Memories of seasons' glow.

Crows of the Abyss

In the ink of the abyss they fly,
Crows on wings of darkest night.
Their calls echo, a ghostly cry,
In realms devoid of light.

They traverse the endless void,
Guardians of forgotten lore.
In the abyss, where hope's destroyed,
Crows flock forevermore.

Their eyes, like embers, pierce the dark,
Witnesses to eternal gloom.
Crows of the abyss, their stark,
Presence heralds doom.

Pandemonium Perch

Upon the perch of chaos' reign,
Where shadows dance in wild delight.
There sits a bird of feathered pain,
Pandemonium takes its flight.

With eyes that spark, fierce glowing red,
It seeks the heart's tumultuous drum.
On wings of fury, spirits dread,
A harbinger of what's to come.

In realms where order bends and breaks,
The pandemonium bird declares.
Where madness blooms and reason shakes,
It perches, stoking endless cares.

Eclipse of Shadows

Beneath the ashen sky they meet
Where moon and sun in silence greet
Shadows play their hidden game
In twilight's soft and muted flame

A dance of secrets, slow and deep
Whispers of the night do creep
Through the veil of dark and light
In endless waltz of fleeting sight

The stars observe with patient eyes
As darkness cloaks the world in lies
A hush of wind, a sighing tree
A moment trapped in mystery

The shadows chase the fleeting spark
Boundaries fade into the dark
Silence holds the breath of time
In cosmic riddle, pure and prime

But in this cold and tender hold
The truth of secrets, brave and bold
Reveals itself in whispered tones
A universe in shadows grown

Wings of Omen

On winds of change the omens ride
With feathers dark as midnight's tide
They circle high, they circle wide
Foretelling tales of fate's abide

Their voices echo through the air
A prophecy in whispers fair
Beneath their gaze, the world does spin
With secrets deep, and shadows thin

In ancient skies their message brought
Of battles lost and victories bought
The future painted on the wing
In cryptic song the omens sing

Their wings, the messengers of night
In moonlit glow, in dim twilight
They carry dreams and fears untold
Of destinies in night enfold

As dawn's first light begins to gleam
Dispelling night's enshrouded dream
The omens fade into the blue
But leave behind a clue, a cue

Guardians of the Lost

In silent woods where shadows crawl
The guardians answer every call
With eyes that pierce the veils of dusk
Secrets old, their task to trust

They wander paths where none may tread
Among the spirits of the dead
Their duty sworn in ancient vows
To shield the lost in sacred bounds

The moon's pale light their only guide
Through forests vast and mountains wide
They keep the lore from ages past
Within their hearts, the die is cast

Whispers of the bygone days
Resonate in ghostly lays
The guardians stand, the lost among
Protecting tales unsaid, unsung

Eternal watch they vigil keep
For lost souls in the darkness steep
A silent vow, a promise made
To shelter all where shadows fade

Feathered Observer

Perched upon an ancient tree,
I watch the world and all I see.
Feathered eyes, so keen and bright,
Peering through the dawn's first light.

From dawn till dusk, I take my place,
Observing life's unhurried pace.
A silent witness to the day,
As shadows lengthen and they sway.

The forest whispers tales of old,
In branches high, in stories told.
Each rustling leaf, a secret shared,
In twilight's hues, I'm always there.

Beneath me, rivers flow and wind,
In nature's grace, a peace I find.
Feathered and flight, yet grounded still,
Observing all with patience, will.

In quietude, I learn my part,
A feathered seed in nature's heart.
With every beat of wings, I say,
I'll watch and guard both night and day.

Prey in the Panorama

In the hush of twilight's bloom,
Shadows dance on the horizon's loom,
Predators bound through the dusky veil,
Nature whispers a primal tale.

Eyes that gleam with ancient fire,
Survival's song, a boundless choir,
Silent strides through meadow's mist,
Echoes of instinct, unresist.

Windswept grasses bend and sway,
Marking paths for night and day,
Footfalls light on midnight's thread,
Ghostly figures, quickly fled.

Stars above in cosmic play,
Watch the dance of hunt and prey,
In the vastness, lives entwine,
Life and death in a timeless line.

Beneath the moon, a silver fan,
Nature plays its endless plan,
In the panorama, wild and free,
Whispers of eternity.

Majesty in Mortality

In the shadowed vale of time,
Mortality, a fleeting rhyme,
Flecks of stardust, hearts of clay,
We wander, then we fade away.

Majesty in every breath,
Even at the touch of death,
Life's parade, a grand display,
Moments bright, then fall to gray.

Ephemeral as the morning dew,
A chance to live, to start anew,
In a tapestry wide and vast,
Beauty held, though it won't last.

Legacies like whispered dreams,
River-fed by fragile streams,
In the end, a final call,
Majesty in rise and fall.

From the soil we are reborn,
New dawn breaking, night forlorn,
In the circle, life and light,
Day and death, both finite.

Eyes in Flight

Across horizons broad and wide,
Wings of freedom, gliding tide,
Eyes sharp-set, with ancient sight,
Boundless journeys, silent flight.

Clouds embrace the wandering soul,
Carving paths through blue and gold,
Gaze that's cast to lands below,
Silent witness to life's flow.

Feathers dance in northern breeze,
Kissed by sun and moonlit seas,
Through the day and through the night,
Eyes in flight, in infinite light.

Wisdom held in soaring arcs,
Stories etched like forest barks,
From the peaks to shaded glen,
Eyes in flight, they roam again.

Eternal skies, a canvas bright,
Painted paths of black and white,
Above the world, so full of life,
Eyes in flight, escaping strife.

Skybound Sentinel

High aloft where gales meet sky,
Sentinels in silence fly,
Watching world with eagle's grace,
Guardians of an airy space.

Through tempest's roar and sunny gleam,
Holding fast to heaven's seam,
Ever mindful, ever brave,
Skybound sentinel, spirits crave.

Twilight drapes the land afar,
Stars take stage as guiding spar,
Wings that whisper ancient lore,
Skybound sentinel, forever more.

Silent shadow, soaring might,
Keeper of the boundless height,
All below, a fleeting sight,
Skybound sentinel in flight.

From dawn's blush to dusk's embrace,
In the vast, unending space,
Eyes are sharp, the heart is free,
Skybound sentinel, eternally.

Eldritch Observer

In shadows deep where secrets lie,
A watcher stirs, with countless eyes.
Its whispers curl through midnight air,
Silent secrets laid bare.

From ancient depths, where silence reigns,
It peers through time's unending chains.
Beneath its gaze, the cosmos trembles,
As darkness deftly it assembles.

Cryptic runes it inscribes in void,
Unseen worlds it does avoid.
Yet in its watch, truths unfold,
Of stories dark, and ages old.

The stars blink out as it peers near,
A presence neither there nor here.
Eldritch visions grip the mind,
In realms of shadows, none may find.

To look upon the hidden face,
Is to embrace the dark embrace.
For watchers see the soul's deep dread,
And in their gaze, are we misled.

From Lofty Perches

From lofty perches high above,
Birds whisper tales of fear and love.
They see the world in varied hues,
As dawn awakes and spreads its news.

The skies unfold a painted scene,
With golden light and emerald green.
Their wings a-flutter, glide with grace,
Upon this endless, vast embrace.

They sing of places far and wide,
Beyond the reach of mortal stride.
Their calls, a melody so pure,
A solace for the hearts unsure.

In quiet storm or gentle breeze,
They feel each whisper of the trees.
They soar through realms that none can cage,
Eternal dancers of this stage.

The freedom found in open skies,
Is mirrored in their knowing eyes.
From lofty perches, they impart,
The simple joys to mend the heart.

Death's Navigator

A boat on streams of spectral light,
Guided by hands both dark and slight.
The ferryman knows not of fear,
His path is clear, his vision sheer.

Through veils of night and whispers low,
He charts the course where shadows go.
Across the river, cold and wide,
To realms where souls in silence bide.

With eyes as deep as endless night,
He steers through fates both dark and bright.
No map he needs, no star he seeks,
For he has heard what deathly speaks.

His cloak as dark as midnight's breath,
Enfolds the tales of endless death.
Yet in his heart there beats a truth,
Of life beyond the final ruth.

In death's embrace, he finds his way,
Through gloom and grace, to break of day.
For he, the guide, the silent friend,
Knows all must cross the river's bend.

Dark Wings

Dark wings beat against twilight sky,
Where shadows dance and night birds fly.
The silent flight of ravens' wings,
Carries the echo of darkened things.

In moonlit glades, where secrets grow,
They perch on branches, row by row.
Their eyes like beacons, sharp and keen,
Reflect the silence crisp and clean.

Whispers carried on the breeze,
Through ancient woods and eldest trees.
The owls' call in the midnight hush,
A lullaby that stirs the brush.

Their flight unseen, yet always near,
They glide through dreams, dispelling fear.
Guardians of the twilight veil,
Intruders of life's whispered tale.

With wings of shadow, hearts of night,
They vanish into morning's light.
Yet their presence lingers on,
In dreams that dance till night has gone.

Hollow Eyes

Beneath the eerie, haunted skies,
There dwell the ones with hollow eyes.
They see the world in shades of grey,
As time just slips and fades away.

Their gaze is void, yet deeply still,
With knowledge formed from ancient will.
Through silent night and endless days,
They wander lost in spectral ways.

No words escape their silent screams,
Their minds entwined with fractured dreams.
They walk the shadows, lost and cold,
With stories left untold, unsold.

Their presence chills the summer air,
A ghostly drift of dark despair.
In hollow eyes, the past remains,
A mirror of long-gone pains.

To meet their gaze is to recall,
The silent echoes of the fall.
For hollow eyes reveal the truth,
Of life's elusive, fleeting youth.

Harbingers of Cleanup

When winter's breath retreats in flight,
And snows dissolve, revealing light,
The harbingers of cleanup show,
To sweep away the last of snow.

With brooms aflash, they clear the street,
Erasing marks of icy sleet,
And blossoms bloom where frost has lain,
Reviving earth from winter's pain.

They sing the song of budding trees,
And whisper to the waking bees,
Ensuring all within their sweep,
Rises from the winter sleep.

Their hands, so deft with tender care,
Restore the lands, make hearts aware,
That spring has come with promises,
To fill the world with fragrant bliss.

The sky, once gray, now bathes in blue,
As harbingers, their work renew,
A new beginning, fresh and bright,
To greet the world with morning light.

Above the Fray

Upon the peaks where eagles soar,
There's solace found and worries no more,
High above the world's display,
Where winds of freedom, ever sway.

The land below, a bustling scene,
Of hurried footsteps, lost routine,
Yet here in skies so vast and clear,
They're murmurs lost, they disappear.

A realm untouched by petty wars,
Where silence speaks, and nature roars,
The clouds, a waltz in azure bloom,
Dispel the earth-bound grip of gloom.

In heights, where thoughts can freely roam,
One finds their heart, their spirit's home,
Above the fray, where peace alights,
The soul unburdened in its flights.

So let us dream of wings we own,
To rise above, be all alone,
Where tranquil winds their secrets say,
In realms of sky, above the fray.

The Grim Survey

Amidst the quiet, shadows play,
Where time has etched its slow decay,
The grim survey, with eyes so cold,
Reveals the tales that stones have told.

The ruins speak of days long gone,
Of battles lost and victories won,
Of laughter turned to silent cries,
Beneath the endless, watchful skies.

Nature reclaims what men forsake,
As ivy wraps around the stake,
And whispers of the past converge,
In echoes that the winds will urge.

Each broken wall, each shattered beam,
Holds memories of someone's dream,
The lives that once here bloomed and thrived,
In ghostly marks, they are revived.

So walk these grounds with quiet tread,
Respect the tales of those once led,
By hopes and fears, through night and day,
Into the past, the grim survey.

Lofted Lords

Upon the castles built in clouds,
The lofted lords look down on crowds,
Their citadels of dream and light,
Enshrouded in the mystic's sight.

They rule the skies with gentle grace,
Detached from earth's unending race,
Their hearts attune to cosmic hymns,
Above the world's ephemeral whims.

Their reign is peace, their sword, a star,
That guides the lost from near and far,
In realms where time holds no domain,
And joy is free from mortal strain.

With whispers soft, they weave the air,
In patterns rich, beyond compare,
Creating worlds of endless dawn,
Where every wish and hope are drawn.

These lofted lords, in silence dwell,
Their secrets, tales of stars to tell,
So gaze above and know they guard,
In realms of light, with vision marred.

Carrion Keepers

In shadows deep where silence weeps,
The keepers of the night do creep,
With eyes aglow, they reap and sow,
Where carrion's secrets softly flow.

Their hunger's call, a voiceless thrall,
In twilight's grip, they softly fall,
Feathers black and talons keen,
Their silent flight remains unseen.

Bones they scatter, dreams they shatter,
In the dark, their wings do matter,
On barren ground and quiet mounds,
In spectral silence, they make rounds.

The moonlit night, their covert right,
Guardians of what's lost from sight,
Echoes past through time they sift,
In carrion's care, the night they lift.

Eternal keepers, secrets sleepers,
Through endless night, they are reapers,
In whispered tones and breathless sigh,
The carrion keepers softly fly.

Circle of Life and Death

Beneath the sun and moon's embrace,
We journey through a timeless chase,
From birth to end, we weave the thread,
In circles spun from life and dread.

The flowers bloom, they greet their doom,
A cycle turning through the gloom,
In every leaf and petal fair,
The breath of death, we see it there.

From cradle care to sorrow's stare,
A dance of fate we all must bear,
In moments brief we share the air,
And then return from whence we flare.

A fleeting touch of warmth we clutch,
In grim embrace or tender hush,
The wheel it turns, and turns again,
In life and death, we find our kin.

Immutable, the endless dance,
In life's embrace, we take our chance,
And though we part, our spirits stay,
In circle's end, we find our way.

Death Watch Daguerreotype

In twilight's glow they stand and pose,
With somber eyes, their stories close,
A frame of stillness, time's disguise,
The daguerreotype before our eyes.

With shadows deep and faces pale,
In silvered light, their secrets trail,
Reflections caught in mercury's hold,
Their silent watch, a tale retold.

The lens of death, it softly weaves,
The final breath through fallen leaves,
In sepia tones, a glimpse we see,
Of lives once lived in used-to-be.

Their whispered past, a fading cast,
In daguerreotype, forever fast,
A picture's grace, in stillness' trace,
Of final thoughts and fleeting face.

In captured light, they find their rest,
A memory's breath, the stillness blessed,
In frames of sorrow, shades so slight,
Their essence holds through endless night.

Skyborne Sentinel

Amidst the clouds and azure high,
A sentinel guards the endless sky,
With wings outstretched and gaze so keen,
A watcher of the unseen.

In silent flight through realms of blue,
It charts a path both vast and true,
Where sun and stars together lie,
The sentinel surveys the sky.

Its feathers catch the morning light,
In balance held, a skyward sight,
Through storms that rage and calm's repose,
The sentinel forever goes.

Above the world in boundless sweep,
Its vigil kept as mortals sleep,
A guardian where dreams are spun,
It soars until the night is done.

With every dawn and sunset's hue,
The skyborne sentinel rings true,
Through endless age and fleeting breeze,
It keeps the watch with tranquil ease.

Flight of the Grim

On ebony wings, despair takes flight,
Through haunted valleys, under moon's glinting light.
Specters whisper tales of sorrow and dread,
In a world where night devours what's said.

Silent cries echo in the dark's embrace,
As shadows dance in this forsaken place.
Stars weep light, hope seemingly lost,
In the chilling grip, of eternal frost.

Grim winds howl, cold as winter's bane,
Souls are drawn to an endless chain.
Midnight drapes its heavy cloak,
Breathless whispers, law unbroke.

Ancient trees sigh, burdened by time,
Their twisted forms speak in riddles and rhyme.
Through the eerie gloom, life seems slim,
Guided by the flight of the Grim.

Silent Summoner

In the heart of shadows, whispers take form,
Summoning spirits, faceless and warm.
Silent the call, deep in the night,
Bringing forth phantoms, to the flickering light.

No words are spoken, no chants are heard,
The summoner's silence, carries the word.
An ancient bond, forged in the dark,
Between life and the spectral spark.

Moonlight cascades on the spectral gathering,
Ghostly forms, in silence, uttering.
Their silent song, a melancholic tune,
Beneath the glare of a watchful moon.

Ethereal beings, bound by silent plea,
Drift through the night, wild and free.
The silent summoner stands still,
Commanding spirits with a sovereign will.

Heaven's Ravenous

Beneath celestial realms, hunger does stir,
Eager jaws of fate, heavens blur.
Stars consumed in ravenous feast,
Light devoured, darkness released.

Galaxies spin in a cosmic spree,
Feeding the void, eternally free.
Nebulae churn, in tempestuous flight,
In the maw of night, no respite.

Constellations tremble, on periphery's edge,
Their celestial joy, turned to dread.
Planets swallowed, in the cosmic strive,
In heaven's hunger, none survive.

Abyssal gulfs, whisper secrets untold,
Of a universe, in a ravenous hold.
Heaven's maw, hungry and grand,
Consumes all, by silent command.

Shadowed Plight

In the alleys of dusk, shadows ensnare,
Whispering woes in the frigid air.
Silent steps tread in paths so dark,
Bearing burdens, a sorrowful mark.

Gloom weaves tales of forgotten lore,
In corners where light exists no more.
Echoes of grief, in silence they roam,
Seeking solace in twilight's home.

Veils of night conceal the plight,
In realms where day surrenders to night.
Whispers of woe, carried aloft,
By winds that blow, subtle and soft.

Cloaked figures drift in somber flight,
Bound to the realm of eternal night.
In shadow's hold, their spirits fight,
Endlessly trapped in a shadowed plight.

Dark Feathered Witness

In twilight's soft and somber hue,
A shadow watches, still and true.
Its eyes observe the world below,
Where secrets dwell and whispers flow.

A cloak of night upon its wings,
The silent owl, a host it sings.
To mysteries both old and near,
It sees through darkness, without fear.

Echoes of an ancient past,
In moonlit eyes, the memories cast.
Silent guardian of the mind,
The dark-feathered, wise, and kind.

Upon the branch, a witness keen,
To sights both sacred and unseen.
The world beneath its steady gaze,
Unfolds in shadows, night displays.

When morning breaks and light is due,
The feathered watcher bids adieu.
With grace, it fades into the grey,
Awaiting night, to watch, to stay.

Airborne Harbinger

From distant clouds, a herald flies,
With wings that cut through vast blue skies.
Its call precedes the storm's advance,
A prelude to the tempest's dance.

In circling paths, it rides the gale,
The wind its chariot swift and pale.
A voice that echoes through the air,
Of change to come, a world's affair.

With feathers dark as stormy night,
It glides on currents strong and bright.
An omen of the shift to be,
In nature's grand, eternal sea.

The earth below, it scans with care,
For signs of life, for signs of dare.
Its presence speaks of nature's might,
In fleeting glimpses, pure delight.

As storms do rage and skies do weep,
The harbinger remains in sweep.
A touchstone 'midst the wild array,
Guiding hearts through night and day.

Beak and Solitude

In silence, perched upon the high,
A raven's call cuts through the sky.
Its voice, a mark of solitude,
In lonely spaces, thoughts intrude.

A sentinel in feathered guise,
With beak that speaks and eyes so wise.
It ponders all in quiet flight,
The day, the dusk, the falling night.

The world below moves fast and bold,
Yet it remains, a story told.
In flight, it finds a somber peace,
In perches tall, a sweet release.

Companion to the still and calm,
It weaves a life, a silent psalm.
A guardian of solitude,
In open air, in quietude.

The raven's tale, a whispered song,
Of lands where it does not belong.
In solitude, it finds a home,
In skies so vast, it roams, it roams.

Wind's Reaper

Upon the wind, a figure glides,
With wings that stretch the open tides.
A reaper of the skies so vast,
On currents wild, it travels fast.

Its feathers black, a cloak in flight,
It rides the winds both day and night.
A specter in the airy expanse,
That moves with grace, a weightless dance.

In search of something yet untold,
It sifts through skies a thousandfold.
A reaper not of death, but air,
Collects the whispers, fleeting, rare.

Wherever breezes softly hum,
The wind's reaper, there it comes.
To gather secrets swept away,
From dawn's first light to end of day.

Invisible yet presence shown,
In shadows cast, in winds full blown.
The reaper dances with the breeze,
In skies above, with soaring ease.